To Claire—
My grieving fiend!
Every Day is a Gift.

—Mako
9/22

To Mary and Bobby,
Marianne thought this was for me. ☺
—Claire♡

Everyone Dies

WRITTEN BY

Marianne Matzo, PhD, FAAN
and Darlene Domanik

EVERYONE DIES

Dedicated to the crab
whose untimely death
inspired this book,
and to Jax, who
asked the question.

WHY THIS BOOK IS IMPORTANT

If you have children in your lives, they may have asked you about dying and death. Your first thought may have been, "Wouldn't you rather know where babies come from?" because that could be a much easier conversation.

Understanding that everyone dies—and why—is a gift we can give the children in our lives so they learn that death is normal. In the past, children saw birth and death on an almost daily basis because they lived in close proximity to these events. That is no longer the case. I have a friend who just turned 70 and both of his parents are still alive; it wasn't until his mid-sixties when he experienced the death of a loved one.

Just as everyone is born, everyone dies. Dying is a normal part of life, and we will witness it before our own deaths. Normalizing death, as is done in this story, helps to lessen the fear of mortality. This book can help a child develop a simple and true understanding of dying and death.

—Marianne Matzo, PhD, FAAN

When I was about five years old, I was taken from home and shuffled between neighbors and family for over a year. I overheard adults say that my mother was dying and I found that idea frightening and confusing. No one explained what was happening—probably because they just didn't know how.

I hope this book gives parents the words they need to open this discussion, and to help their children understand this "fact of life." They will be better prepared to cope when the inevitable occurs.

[Ironically, Mom recovered and lived until age 86.]

—Darlene Domanik

Jax and his grandpa, Pops, found a crab claw on the beach.

"Where is the crab?" Jax asked. "How did his arm come off?"

"It died," Pops answered.

Jax asked, "What does that mean?"

Pops said, "It's when a living thing stops moving, eating, even breathing."

"Will we die?" asked Jax.

"Yes," Pops said. "Everyone dies. It is normal."

Jax asked, "Why?"

4

Pops answered, "People die when they are VERY VERY hurt, like this crab that lost its arm. Or VERY VERY sick, like when Gram died a few years ago. Or when they are VERY VERY old."

"Oh," said Jax. "I cut my finger. It really hurt and bled a lot! I needed stitches and a shot and a bandage. Could I die from that?"

"No," said Pops. "It's when you get so hurt that even the doctor, or medicine or an operation can't fix you."

Jax asked, "Like a big car crash on the road? And the ambulance is there?"

"Yes," said Pops. "Sometimes the doctors can fix people and sometimes they can't."

Jax wondered, "My friend is sick. She has a fever, and her nose runs and she coughs. Will she die?"

"Not now, Jax," Pops answered. "She's not VERY VERY sick. VERY VERY sick is when someone can't get better no matter what. It's when resting, or medicine or even an operation can't help."

Jax looked at Pops. He had gray hair and wrinkles and had lived a long time. "Pops," Jax asked, "Are you VERY VERY old?"

Pops laughed. "I'm old, but not VERY VERY old."

"Will you die?" Jax asked.

"Yes, but hopefully not for a long, long time." Pops said.

"Ok!" said Jax.

They walked back along the beach. Jax saw his dad and showed him the crab claw. Dad asked where the rest of the crab was. "Did he go to his home in the ocean?"

"No," Jax said, "He was VERY VERY hurt, and he died. Did you know, Dad, that everyone dies?"

9

Dad said, "That's true, Jax."

They made a sand castle and put the crab claw on top.
They had such a nice day on the beach.

Pops asked, "Wasn't today fun? Every day is a gift!"

Jax said, "Then let's have fun every day!"

Pops said, "That's a great plan, Jax. I wish everyone thought like you!"

Dad said, "Every day I get to spend with you and Pops is special. I wish I could do this more, but I have a job."

Jax said, "Don't be sad, Dad. We have today! Don't waste any of our time being sad."

So they didn't.

Jax went home to take a nap.
He put the crab claw next to
him in bed.

"What's this?" Mom asked.

13

"It's from a crab who died," Jax said. "Did you know, Mom, everyone dies?"

"Oh dear!" said Mom.

"It's ok," said Jax, "We only die when we are VERY VERY hurt, or VERY VERY sick, or VERY VERY old. It's normal. Until then, we can have fun every day!" Mom asked, "Where did you learn this?"

Jax said, "From Pops."

Mom said, "Pops is VERY VERY wise."

And he was.

He lived a very, very long time,
and so did Jax. And every single
day was a gift that they gave to
each other.

FROM THE AUTHORS

We hope you enjoyed this story and that it leads to a healthy, age-appropriate discussion on this important topic. Marianne and Darlene will soon offer another book suitable for school aged children.

ACKNOWLEDGEMENTS

Marianne and Darlene thank Colleen Gleason, our successful author friend who has championed this project since the very beginning.

They thank their editors Erin Wolfe and Winifred Motherwell, retired clinical psychologist Greg Gavrilides, and all our family and friends who read earlier versions to their children. They are grateful for the patience and continuing support of their spouses, David Gillett and Gary March.

Last but not least, they thank Marianne and David's grandson Jax, whose afternoon on the beach inspired this story.

ABOUT THE AUTHORS

Marianne Matzo earned her PhD [1996] in Gerontology. As a certified nurse practitioner in oncology and palliative care, she dedicated her 44-year career in nursing to pain and symptom management for people living with incurable illnesses. A retired university professor, Marianne is now focusing on community education regarding dying and death. This book is the latest creative project on which Marianne and Darlene have collaborated during their 60-year friendship.

Darlene Domanik, JD [1982] is a retired environmental lawyer and childcare advocate. In retirement she owned/managed two childcare facilities serving approximately 500 children. A child at heart, she can entertain an entire room full of toddlers with nothing other than a blanket. She is presently a meditation teacher, artist, and community activist in her hometown of Brighton, Michigan.

CPSIA information can be obtained
at www.ICGtesting.com
Printed in the USA
BVHW022137130321
602168BV00001B/1

9 781944 665654